ON THE INSIDE LOOKING OUT

THE AFTERMATH OF A TORNADO...

LIVING WITH PTSD

Connie Owens

Acknowledgements

I would like to express my gratitude to my therapist, Karla Jeffreys, LPC, LPCS, for encouraging me to share my experience and write about it in the hope that others may better understand PTSD. I could not have made it through this ordeal without you. It has been and continues to be a long and difficult journey.

I want to give a very special thank you to my sister, Cheryl, for saving my life! Your phone calls that day made all the difference. You are why I am here today!

Thank you, David Sawyer and the WNCT Storm Team, for alerting everyone that the tornado was near and dangerous!

Thank you so much, Brad. You are truly my hero. You rescued me within minutes of this catastrophe. I will never forget your strength and thoughtfulness!

Thanks to my nephew, Thomas, for being there first and for coordinating all the volunteers to salvage what we could.

Thanks to my best friend, Jackie, for being there to listen, to offer words of encouragement, and for not giving up on me. Thank you, also, for reading this book at least 100 times and helping with edits!

Thanks to all my family, friends, and co-workers, who provided equipment, storage, muscle power, and support. Each and everything you did helped me endure this ordeal.

Last but not least, I wish to express a sense of gratitude and love to my sister, Marsha, and brother in law, Tommy, for their manual support, emotional support, strength, a place to live, and for everything you did to help me endure the darkest days of my life.

Preface

An EF3 tornado hit Snow Hill, North Carolina, at 5:55 p.m. on Saturday, April 16, 2011. I was there. I was inside it. I witnessed what most people never will, but I survived... physically that is.

The National Weather Service reported that this tornado was 400 yards wide and 18 miles long with sustained winds from 145 to 160 miles per hour. It was one of twelve tornadoes associated with three super cell thunderstorms in eastern North Carolina on this date. It was the worst tornado outbreak in North Carolina history, totalling 31 with 16 rated as EF2 and EF3.

Many people think Post Traumatic Stress Disorder is an imaginary disorder, symptoms that people invent. Trust me; it is not. Here is my story, and I hope after you read it that you will better understand the effect that trauma can impose on a person's mind, changing them forever. I never dreamed my life would be affected like this, but it is... and continues to be.

Symptoms of PTSD

Intrusive, upsetting memories of the event

Flashbacks (reliving the traumatic event)

Nightmares (upsetting dreams)

Avoiding activities you once enjoyed

Loss of interest in activities/ life in general

Feeling detached or estranged from others

Emotionally numb

Hopelessness about the future

Difficulty falling asleep or staying asleep

Irritability, agitation, or outbursts of anger

Difficulty in concentrating

Hypervigilance (on constant "red alert")

Feeling jumpy or easily startled

Difficulty maintaining close relationships

Memory problems

Table of Contents

Dedicated to Mama

Chapter 1: The Day From Hell

April 16, 2011, is a date that I will never forget. It was a Saturday, and I was doing household chores and other things that I would normally do on the weekend. I had just come back the day before from a week of vacation to Myrtle Beach so I had a lot of laundry to wash and catching up to do. I needed to rest before going back to work on Monday.

I had my morning coffee, got the washer and dryer going, vacuumed, swept floors, dusted the furniture, cleaned bathrooms, and went to the grocery store. When I returned, I put away the groceries and decided to kick back and watch a movie to unwind. I caught the end of a WNCT news special and saw where a tornado had touched down and destroyed a Lowe's hardware store in Sanford, NC. The pictures were very dramatic, and I thought it must be extremely powerful to cause so much damage. I continued to flip through the channels and found a good movie to watch. I was relaxing; little did I know I was going to need it.

My sister, Cheryl, called me around 3:00 p.m. to ask if I was looking at the news and weather. I replied, "No, I'm watching a movie." She suggested that I might want to keep an eye on the tornado that was coming across North Carolina. In the back of my mind, I thought this thing was travelling north and not toward me at all. I also thought that tornadoes jump and do not maintain constant contact with the ground in a continuous pattern. That would be a wrong conclusion. I switched back over, watched the local news for a few minutes, and saw the tornado activity near me, but I still thought it would veer north.

Cheryl called again at 5:40 p.m. and said, "Turn on Channel 9. The tornado is getting close to Snow Hill. You need to get in your safe place!" I told her that I would. I looked outside and it was sunny with no sign of anything unusual happening, but I did go out and bring in my American flag from the front porch. When I watched the news bulletin just a few minutes later, the meteorologist said, "This tornado is dangerous. It is on the ground. If you are within this red square, seek shelter right away. If you have a football helmet, a bicycle helmet, or a motorcycle helmet, put it on because there will be a lot of debris flying around." I was definitely inside that red square, and it caught my attention. At the same time Cheryl texted me, "GET IN YOUR SAFE PLACE NOW!"

Chapter 1: The Day From Hell

(Photo by Jeff Hill)

The actual tornado minutes before it hit me

I went through the motorcycle stage a few years ago. Later I sold the bike, but kept all the leather coats, boots, helmet, and other paraphernalia. Very casually I put my helmet on, stood in front of the mirror, and snapped a picture of myself... almost in a humorous gesture. I then texted Cheryl, attached the picture, and typed, "I'm tornado ready!" Little did I know that was a very incorrect statement, and I should not be joking around. I even went to the kitchen and mixed myself a shot of Cherry Vodka and Red Bull (a cherry bomb) to take the edge off in case the storm got a little messy.

I took this picture joking that I was tornado ready

By this time it was 5:50 p.m., and I began to hear the wind pick up. I looked outside, and the 12-foot tall red-tip shrubs on both sides of my property were blown over bent to the ground, but in *OPPOSITE* directions! I said, "Oh crap!" At that point I thought the tornado must be really close. I was suddenly overcome by an overwhelmingly thick, almost nauseating fragrance of pine, and there was no doubt in my mind whatsoever, it's here!

Someone told me once, "If you ever hear of a tornado coming your way and you smell pine, take shelter immediately because it is coming directly toward you." This happens when a tornado clips the tops out of pine trees and the pine oil causes the smell. I instantly went to the walk-in closet in my master bathroom, cell phone in hand, grabbed a pillow to hug, closed the door, and sat down.

As the wind intensified, it sounded like pine cones, small tree limbs, and other debris began to hit the house. A weird noise in the distance was getting louder and louder. All of a sudden it sounded and felt like a big truck rammed full speed into the rear of my house. Immediately following that jolt, it sounded like someone with a machine gun was outside unloading on me. My whole house was shaking like crazy, and I began to panic!! At first I thought one of the tall pine trees in my back yard had fallen on the house, but then the house lifted; yes, lifted! Then it dropped back down. Then it lifted again (I felt like I was floating) and dropped me for the second time. I was screaming, "Dear God, help me!" After letting out a string of obscenities, I went back to praying.

The noise was unbearable. My ears were popping like on an airplane, but much worse. It felt as if the air was being sucked out of my lungs and that sound... there is no way to accurately describe the sound that it was making. Some say a tornado sounds like a freight train, but this sound had a higher pitch... more like a jet engine... right beside my head... at full throttle. I began to scream and was terrified beyond belief. I prayed aloud, "God, please, no! Not today... not like this!"

Crazy thoughts were going through my mind. I thought of my daughter, my grandchildren, my mama, my sisters, my family, and my friends. Would I ever see them again? How would they handle the news of my dying? How would this affect their lives? What minute would I die? What would the news say about this tragedy? It is amazing what goes through your mind when you are on the brink of death.

Chapter 1: The Day From Hell

All of a sudden part of my roof blew off, my closet door flew open, and a stream of water was shooting out of my commode from the suction. Then the commode shot up out of the floor. An assortment of western boots stored on the top shelf of my closet were flying out one by one through the skylight in my bathroom ceiling, and things were falling on me and hitting me on the head. Thank God I had on the helmet. On the shelf above me were a big jar filled with collectible marbles and a big jug filled with pocket change. Both of them fell on me, and there were obvious dings in the helmet from the blows. The suction was pulling on me harder and harder, but luckily, two closet rods full of clothes fell across each other and pinned me underneath the weight. It continued to pull on me, sucking my tennis shoes off my feet in swift motion. I began to scream and pray more and more. I knew this was it... it is almost over... the end for Connie! I never knew a tornado had such suction power! I believe that is what causes the most damage.

Sounds were loud and frightening as if I was in a horror movie... the horror movie from hell! Metal grinding, glass breaking, wood twisting and snapping, wind howling, and unimaginable weird noises resounded. More crazy thoughts went through my mind. Is today the day I die? Is this the way I die? Will it hurt? Will it be quick? Will I suffer? Will I be sucked up and disappear? What does it feel like to be dead? Will my body ever be found? I thought of The Wizard of Oz and wondered if I was floating in the air like Dorothy. Then I felt an overwhelming calm as if God Himself were there, holding me and reassuring me that I was not alone. I accepted my fate at that moment, and I was *okay* with this being the end for me. I was scared beyond belief but not scared to die. That was a very strange feeling.

Suddenly my house lifted up a third time, shook violently, and dropped again. When it lifted a fourth time, I felt like I was blasted out of a cannon with the most powerful g-force you can imagine. It dropped me hard this time, and I could hear the sound begin to move away from me, farther and farther away, and then just dead silence.

Exhausted and injured, I lay there with debris and clothing piled on top of me. My heart was about to pound out of my chest. That last drop really jarred my body, and now I was hurting. I was trembling with fright, wondering was this it, or would there be more? I wondered, "Am I dead? Is this what it's like?"

I could not move from being pinned under all the debris. I somehow managed to hold on to my cell phone throughout the entire ordeal. I could move my right hand enough to press the send button to call the last person I had spoken to... Cheryl. She answered, but we could barely hear each other because my phone was still connected to my Bluetooth, wherever in the world it might be! After I called her three times and we could not hear each other, I manipulated the phone from underneath all the clutter and pressed the buttons to disconnect the Bluetooth. When I called her the fourth time, we were connected and could hear each other. I told her I needed help, that I had been hit hard and was pinned in my house. She asked, "Are you joking or is this real?" When I told her it was no joke, she said she could hear the fear in my trembling voice. Then she panicked. She said she danced in place as she told me to hold on and she would get help to me. Then we disconnected, and I have never felt so alone or scared in my life. Cheryl's family lives about 45 minutes away.

Dead calm loomed everywhere except for my heartbeat sounding extremely loud at that moment. Next I thought I heard something else and got scared. Then I unexpectedly felt someone touch my foot, and I began to scream, "HELP ME!" It was my next-door neighbor, Brad. His house had been hit as well; but when he saw my house, he told his wife, "I have to go check on her. She's home, and she may be hurt!" He said he thought I was dead when he saw my feet under all the rubble until he heard me scream. He helped pull the debris off me and got me to my feet. My legs were like Jell-O, and I could hardly stand. I asked him how bad it was because I was still thinking a tree fell on me. He said, "It's pretty bad, but you aren't the only one." When I looked around, I could not believe my eyes. My beautiful house was demolished. My tennis shoes had been sucked off my feet and disappeared, and debris was knee deep. Brad helped me get out of the closet and over all the broken glass and destruction. When I got to where my dining room and living room should be, there were no walls and no roof. Most of the furniture was outside or completely gone, and what remained was broken. My china was broken and scattered everywhere. When I looked outside, nothing looked right. I asked him, "Where am I?" He stated, "You're still in your yard, but turned different."

Chapter 1: The Day From Hell

The first thing I saw was a picture of Mama lying on a pile of broken wood that was once part of my living room wall. I said, "Hey, Mama, I'm okay!"

The tornado had picked up my house, thrown it 150 ft. off the foundation, and turned it sideways in my yard! Totally disoriented, I looked across the road and saw that my neighbor's house was destroyed. Then I saw some movement over there, and they started crawling out from under the rubble! He shouted, "Are you OKAY? " I shouted back, "I think so; how about you guys?" He responded that they were okay.

My house is top left

It looked like a huge bomb had been dropped. The trees were gone, houses were gone, and nothing looked the same. Our peaceful and quiet community had been wiped off the face of the earth. My other neighbors lived in a singlewide mobile home, and it was totally gone! GONE! They told me later that they had heard the noise, looked out the back door, and jumped out just before the tornado took the whole house away. They were outside in the yard during all this, severely injured but alive. How could any of us survive such disaster and turmoil? Why did we survive when people in other parts of the state did not?

I told Brad I kept a pair of yard shoes in my entryway. He crawled back inside and sure enough, there they were, right where they should be. Thank goodness for that because I was barefooted and could not move an inch in any direction. The temperature outside was much cooler, and I was freezing. I saw a jacket stuck in the debris so I pulled it out, shook off the dirt, and put it on.

Chapter 1: The Day From Hell

Minutes after the tornado hit

My house was sitting here, now 150 ft. away!

Chapter 2: Help Starts Arriving

Cheryl had contacted my nephew, Thomas, to come and assist me. He has been a volunteer firefighter for many years. Thomas and one of his best friends, Michael, who is a flight nurse, were there within minutes. They had trouble getting to me because of debris on the roads, but they got as close as they could and ran the rest of the way, jumping over trees and power lines. Thomas could not believe what he was seeing and ran up and hugged me. I was not alone any longer. I had family there.

I was in shock and remained in shock for several days. I had a bad gash on my right hip, bruises, cuts and scrapes, pieces of glass in my arms and legs, and my back hurt. I refused to go to the hospital. I could not imagine going to the emergency room on a Saturday night at any time, especially today. Moreover, I just could not leave all my *stuff,* or what was left of it. Things were scattered everywhere. Some were mine, and some were my neighbor's. Some were things that belonged to people we did not even know or know how they arrived here, and some were things that we did not recognize what they were. Among other things, I had autographed photos and music memorabilia now scattered to the winds that could never be replaced. Where did it go from here? Is somebody looking at it in his or her yard wondering who owns this?

Within minutes of the tornado, rescue trucks, firefighters, police, EMT's, neighbors, family, and friends started arriving to assist those in need. In the meantime, my nephew had called his mama, my other sister, Marsha. She and her husband, Tommy, live near Kinston, and it took a while for them to drive. They had a difficult time getting through to me because of downed trees and power lines. They had to take a different route because rescue would not let people come through. Marsha could not believe what she saw and she was not prepared for all this. She knew it was bad but had never seen anything like this! When she got to me, she hugged me, and we both got emotional.

Then somebody shouted out, "Another tornado is coming!" I thought," My God.....I have no house to get in!" Then I saw my beautiful convertible Pontiac Solstice, nose down in the ditch, smashed like a tin can. So I thought, "Well, I can't get in the ditch either, so what will I do?" Then someone else shouted, "False alarm!" Thank goodness for that.

Thomas arrives to help

Marsha and I survey the damage

By now it was about 7:00 p.m. and was starting to get dark. The skies were looking angry again, and we did not know if more bad weather was coming our way. We agreed to go back to Marsha and Tommy's house for the night and come back early in the morning. I really did not want to go but had nowhere safe to stay out of the weather. The firefighters and police promised us they would keep people out and keep an eye on things.

Chapter 2: Help Starts Arriving

Cheryl and her husband, Doug, finally made it to Marsha's house around 9:00 p.m. They had to wait until two tornadoes passed their area in Beulaville, NC. Cheryl said she thought they were going to be hit by a tornado also, but it went in another direction. All the sisters and brothers-in-law were together now.

Chapter 3: Shock Sets In

I have no memory of that night. Everyone was shocked about what had happened and very concerned for me. My sisters say they doctored the cut on my butt, and we joked about it. I vaguely remember all that. I also do not remember going back to my house the next day. I have seen photographs of the many friends and family members who came to help save what we could of clothes, furniture, photographs, music equipment, or anything of significance. They came with trucks, trailers, a backhoe, chain saws, rakes, boxes, tape, etc., and did not mind giving up their Sunday to help me. Why can't I remember all that? For days they packed and hauled things to storage for me, and most of it was wet, full of dirt or debris, or broken. A family friend, Mickey, told them to take it all to his garage until I had time to go through it. They say I walked around in a daze, and I must have because I remember very little. My mind was protecting me from all this drama and pain, I guess, and I was zoned out.

My damaged piano goes to storage

Chapter 3: Shock Sets In

For the next week and a half, I went there every day, digging through debris, looking for ANYTHING that was mine. My best friend, Jackie, came and stayed several days to help me. A team of airmen from the 334th Aircraft Maintenance Unit at Seymour-Johnson Air Force base in Goldsboro volunteered through the Red Cross. They brought chainsaws and strong backs and helped clean my yard of all the debris and downed trees. They cut up trees and filled the front-end loader and Jackie would move the debris to a pile by the road. These young men were great and left a lasting impression on me. They worked tirelessly to assist someone they did not know and possibly would never meet again. They all said it meant a lot to them because they would want someone to help their family if they were in need.

On The Inside Looking Out

The 334th Aircraft Maintenance Unit, Jackie, and I

Jackie on the front-end loader

Chapter 3: Shock Sets In

While going through the debris and cutting limbs to prepare for the front-end loader, one of the young men found a piece of cloth with some needlepoint stitched on it. He immediately brought it to me and said, "I know this must be important to someone. I would think it is a treasure to some family." It had the names of a man and woman and their 1940's wedding date. It was nasty but still intact. It appeared to have been framed, but of course, the frame was gone now. I said I would find out who owned it. A good friend of mine, Trudy, who was born and raised in Greene County, happened to stop by that day. I asked her if she had a clue who the owner might be. Her eyes started to water and she stated, "Yes, I know exactly who it is!" She was happy to return it to them and told me later that they were so excited to get it back. Of all the things they lost, this was one of the items they had hoped to recover. Their daughter, Connie, who has passed away, made this for them. It was odd that it landed in the yard of someone named *Connie*. Sentimental items seemed to be the most important to everyone. I am so glad the airman brought it to me and knew it must be important to someone. I cannot say enough about how helpful and how respectful these young men from Seymour-Johnson Air Force Base were.

Some of the most amazing things happen during a tornado. Pictures are sucked out of picture frames, but the frame stays on the wall. Nearly everything was sucked out of my refrigerator, even the icemaker, yet two eggs lay in the debris unharmed. The rack in my dishwasher was sitting in the middle of the room, yet none of the dishes were broken. It even sucked the butter out of the tub and slammed it on the wall. I kept seeing something gray sliding down a wall and wondered, "What in the heck is that?" I then realized it was butter covered with this gray matter that was on everything in sight. Some things were sitting exactly where they were before all this drama, yet other things were gone forever or destroyed. My flat-screen TV was still hanging on the wall, still intact, without a scratch on it. Several items that were previously stored inside the refrigerator mysteriously appeared inside of the wall oven.

For some odd reason I was constantly drawn back to the closet I was trapped in. I could not help it; I could NOT stay away from it. Was it because that is where I almost died? Was it because that is where I felt God's presence? Was it because that is where I lost ME? Why? I suppose it is like people going back to the scene of an accident where someone died simply to be near where they drew their last breath. I know a part of me died that day. Was I grieving? Was I looking for ME? That closet possessed me!

I was buried in this closet

For the following few weeks, I was on the phone with insurance companies, FEMA, and the Red Cross, trying to get everything settled. I found out quickly that FEMA could not assist me. They said I made too much money. Gosh, I certainly did not think that. The insurance companies settled quickly and put some money in my hands to start over. My job was gracious enough to allow me to be out of work by using all my vacation time, plus days without pay, but with an excused absence for three weeks.

Employees at my job passed around an envelope and collected money for me. Churches sent money, friends sent money, and perfect strangers would stop by and give money. The Red Cross was there every day delivering hot meals, water, ice, and snacks. Please, everyone... support your Red Cross. They are great! I felt guilty taking all the handouts. That sure does something to your pride. But I knew I needed it, and it made me feel good to know there are still more good people than bad in this world.

Daily we would use pitchforks or rakes to go through the debris to look for anything salvageable. The remaining structure was knee deep in insulation combined with wet debris blown in by the tornado. Everything in my refrigerator had begun to rot and was smelling awful, but we had to keep searching. We wore face masks and gloves. A news reporter stopped by and asked how it was going. I told her that we just had to keep digging through trash to find treasures. She put my story in her newspaper.

Inside the refrigerator

Searching for anything useful in piles of rubble

Chapter 4: The Good And The Bad

There was a young woman, Ashley, who was looking at the news on TV. She felt compelled to do something to help. She came by every day with sandwiches, small packs of pain relievers, ice, sodas, pizza, or whatever she could acquire by donation. She and I bonded pretty quickly, and she made it a point to come see me every day I was there. When she saw all the guys from Seymour-Johnson, she said that she would bring enough to feed everyone the next day. She arrived as promised the following day with a large pan of baked spaghetti that a restaurant had donated to her. She is one very special young woman.

Even when there is good, there is bad. The looters started coming around like vultures. Tommy was there early one morning to get what was left of my crushed lawn mower and some other things he could load on a trailer. He found three people rummaging around inside, and one of them was taking the breakers out of my electrical panel box! Tommy asked them what they were doing, and they stated they heard the houses were going to be demolished and hauled off. They wanted to see if anything was still there that they could use. Is that some nerve or what? Tommy told them there was nothing there for them and they needed to leave, so they did. I was livid when I found out strangers had been rummaging in my stuff! I found a can of spray paint and sprayed *NO TRESPASSING* and *KEEP OUT* on the outside wall of my house. I was furious to think someone had that kind of nerve. This *junk* is mine! It is all I have left in the world. Please do not take that from me!

They wanted to steal these breakers out of the panel box

Countless people stopped by and asked if they could get things out of the ditches that were broken or demolished. People came by looking to make money by offering tree cutting service, demolition, yard work, and even prayer--- for a fee of course. Fortunately I didn't need their services, thanks to the good-hearted people who genuinely wanted to *help* those in need, be they stranger or friend. They were good people who didn't want to take advantage of the situation or try to make a buck from the misfortune of others. Several church groups stopped by to pray, offering supplies and gift cards.

There was a constant flow of gawkers riding by taking pictures, pointing, and looking. Someone yelled out, "I saw you on TV!" Different crews were coming by asking for interviews or a story for newspapers and television. With cameras rolling (and I'm looking like crap, as you can imagine, with no makeup, wrinkled clothes, wrapped up in dirt, and distraught) most of these stories aired on national TV. A friend in London even saw me on TV! Geez! None of that really bothered me so much because, after all, tornadoes do not happen every day around here. I certainly was not alone in my disheveled appearance. All the destruction had to be interesting to see, and most of the people were compassionate. I probably would have been doing the same thing had it not happened to me. It is truly an odd phenomenon in our neck of the woods.

TV interview

Chapter 5: Letting Go Of The Past

The insurance company sent someone out to get my Pontiac Solstice. It was bowed and shaped like a boomerang when he pulled it out of the ditch and placed it on the trailer to haul off. That really hurt my feelings. Even a TV camera operator had to compose himself before he could film it wrecked in the ditch. He said, "That car is too sweet to look like that!"

I really got emotional on the day the guy came to get my Geo Tracker. I bought that car brand new in 1990 and drove it for years. It had been parked for about two years but was still insured, thank goodness! When he left my driveway with the car on the rollback, I felt it coming. I could feel my body start to shake. I started to cry and could not stop. This was the first time I had cried during this entire ordeal; the first time I really let myself go and just cry. Everyone was telling me it would happen, and on this day it all came apart at the seams. I was all by myself and thought, 'There goes the last thing I own. I have nothing now.' It was pretty overwhelming to say the least.

I was saving that car to give to my older grandson, Mitchell, on his 16th birthday in July. I told Mitchell later, "It doesn't look like you will be getting the Tracker after all, buddy." He understood. I was so sad.

Before and after pictures of Geo Tracker

Before and after pictures of Pontiac Solstice

Chapter 6: Demolition Day

Cheryl found a man who would demolish what remained of my home. The county said that if we put all the debris in the ditch in front of our homes that the state would haul it off for us. Cheryl said she knew if we did not get it done that I would continue to go over there every day. We sat across the road on the embankment that day and watched as he demolished the remnants of my home with an excavator. You can just imagine the emotion of watching your home ripped apart, crushed, and dumped in a ditch. It was strange that as he maneuvered around demolishing the home, the last thing torn down was the closet that I was buried in! He knew nothing of that closet... Nothing. It still possessed me! I had the opportunity to see it one last time before it was crushed and dumped.

Now I have nothing. The only thing left was an empty lot. My house was gone. My cars were gone. My furniture was gone. My landscaped property was gone. A lifetime of working and paying for necessities and treasures was gone. Even my mind was gone, but I did not realize it yet.

The closet, the last thing demolished

A lifetime of memories gone

Chapter 6: Demolition Day

On the day of the tornado, I paused to bring my American flag inside for protection. As a proud American and a patriot of our Great Nation, I always fly my flag. I have a guest bedroom in my home decorated with patriotic memorabilia in red, white, and blue. In 2001, I wrote and recorded a song entitled "I Pledge Allegiance" because I strongly disagreed with removing the words *Under God* from the Pledge. My daddy served with The Big Red One during WWII. My brother and several other close relatives have also served in our military. We are proud to be a patriotic family. Shortly after the tornado was all over, I shoved that flagpole into a big hole that was ripped in the side of my house where it was proudly displayed, tattered and torn, until the day of demolition.

Proudly displaying my American flag

When the property was cleared, Cheryl took a picture of me with the flag. I wanted it to fly at my new home one day. It was my pledge to keep it flying, and it did until it finally fell apart. I have since replaced it with a new flag, but I still have this one.

Standing on an empty lot, nothing left but my flag

Chapter 7: Beginning To Fall Apart

Moving forward: after weeks of red tape and headaches, all insurance claims were settled. The house was demolished and gone. I was temporarily living with my sister, Marsha, and brother-in-law, Tommy. I began the task of trying to find a new house. I knew I could not rebuild where I was previously living. There were too many bad memories. I sold that property to Brad and Amanda next door. He was my hero for pulling me out of my house that day. I am glad I could sell to them.

I had problems sleeping from the very first night. The simplest sound would cause me to jump out of my skin. My nerves were terrible, and my ability to concentrate was zero. I could not remember things, and depression set in. I felt thrown away. I had no home; no sanctuary; no place to just go and *be*. I felt like a bag lady. I felt worthless and useless. The loneliness was constant and overwhelming. I missed *my stuff.* I had always taken pride in keeping a neat, organized house and could readily put my finger on everything I owned. Now what little I had left was stored in boxes in several locations, and I did not even know what was or was not in the boxes. I remained in my room by myself every night. I would eat supper with Marsha and Tommy and then go to my room. They were great to me and were very understanding. They did not probe into my business. They just listened if I needed to talk or tell them something. Marsha would ride with me to look at houses as I researched the market. I found a realtor who was most anxious to help me find a home. We would go look at houses two or three times a week. Then Marsha and I would discuss the pros and cons and decide to keep looking. I saw a few homes that I liked, but they just did not feel right.

I went back to work in June, and I knew my life would never be the same. I became the *tornado lady*. People would stop by my desk and introduce me as "She's the lady who was in the tornado." This happened time after time after time, and I realized this would be my fate. People would stop by and ask questions about it all. What was it like? What did it look like? What did it sound like? I know people are curious, but I really did not want to talk about it day after day. It was already there, already constantly on my mind ALL the time. Then there were the jokesters who would say, "Hey, that tornado warning didn't get to you last night, did it?" They would laugh. People treated me differently; maybe because I WAS different. I am different. I know this.

In a couple of weeks, I had a mini-meltdown at work. I just could not deal with the people, the questions, the whispers, and the *look*. You know the look people have when their eyes say, "Oh, poor thing. She is the tornado lady. She lost everything, and she has nothing." It happened every time I walked into a room or passed by someone... and I detested it. I was ready to walk out of there and never go back.

One of the upper-level managers heard that I was not doing well. He came by my desk and said, "Come walk with me." He told me to take some time away from work. He said that I had been through more in a couple of months than most could tolerate in a lifetime, and he didn't know how I was holding up as well as I had. He said he would work out my absences. I had used all my vacation time, so I got time off without pay again, but with excused absences. He also suggested that I call our Employee Assistance Program, and they could refer me to a therapist. I really did not want to go to a *shrink* because it was like giving in to it, but he thought it might help. I have always been the strong, independent one in the family, and my pride would not let me admit that I needed help. I continued to think that time would heal me, and I would begin to recover *tomorrow.* Sadly, tomorrow never came.

Chapter 8: Realizing I Need Therapy

After a week and a half off, I went back to work and called the Employee Assistance Program. I told them my story, and they referred me to Goldsboro Counseling Center, P.A., in Goldsboro, NC, and to my therapist, Karla Jeffreys. We began my sessions.

We discussed everything that had happened, I told Karla that I knew I had changed. I did not like to do the things I used to do anymore. I did not really like being around people, crowds terrified me, and I had lost my passion for music. My nerves were completely shot. My senses of touch, hearing, and smell, were all amplified off the scale. My startle response was ridiculous, and I had panic attacks most days. I just could not sleep.

I told her any sound would make me jump out of my skin. I always monitored the weather, nearly obsessed by it, and had acquired an inherent fear that it was coming back for me. That is how I felt! Even ordinary rainy days would throw me for a spin just wondering if the weather would get worse. I began to distance myself from family and friends, making up every excuse I could think of to avoid any situation that required me to *act* as if everything was okay when I knew it was not. I was falling apart, and they did not need to know. Going to work every day and *pretending* I was okay was exhausting me. "Normal" for me was a thing of the past.

We discussed the day of the tornado, the horror and fear I went through, and how I have felt since. She said I was suffering from Post Traumatic Stress Disorder. She asked why I waited so long before seeking help, and I told her I hated to admit I was having problems. She said it was normal to feel that way but was glad I finally reached out for help. She set up visits to her office twice a month and referred me to her staff psychiatrist who would prescribe meds for me. It felt good to finally have someone to talk to about it and help explain it to me. In retrospect, I wish I had gone sooner.

Chapter 9: PTSD Is Changing My Life

In September of 2011, a hurricane was on its way to eastern North Carolina... and Connie was on her way to western North Carolina or points beyond in search of blue skies. I knew I could not go through it, so I disappeared. The fear that was building up in me almost made me sick. I drove 100 miles to Jackie's house, and we escaped down Interstate-85 southwest bound. We drove as far as Winston-Salem, NC, before we saw friendly skies. We spent the night there. The potential hurricane turned north, we were out of harm's way, and headed back home the next day. We made this trip for no other reason than to avoid what *might* happen.

After searching for a house for months without much progress, the woman passed away who lived next door to Marsha. A neighbor told her son that I was trying to find a house to buy so he called me. We made an appointment for me to see it, and I knew immediately that this was the house I wanted. I had made an offer and was waiting for approval on the mortgage when the aforementioned hurricane forced me to escape to points west. I was very worried during the trip that the hurricane had damaged the house so I called Marsha to find out the local situation. She assured me there was no damage, just some trees down and a lot of debris.

During the drive back from Winston-Salem, the damage appeared worse as I got closer to home. I wondered if Marsha had only told me it was slight damage so I would not panic. Sure enough, it was exactly as she said... trees down and debris. The thought ran through my mind, 'I already lost one home to a tornado. Please don't let me lose another one to a hurricane before I even get moved into it!'

After finishing details and closing on my house, in October of 2011, I drove home. As I turned down the long road to my house, what did I see? A rainbow!! It was hanging in the sky literally pointing at my new house. I stopped in the middle of the road, and with tears in my eyes, I took this picture.

A rainbow guides me home

It was strange yet comforting to see that rainbow, and I cannot describe the feeling that came over me. It was as if God was giving me a sign that everything was going to be alright, that I was home and He would keep me safe. I also thought maybe it was the previous owner saying, "Welcome home!"

I immediately began remodeling. All the planning and activity kept my hands and mind busy for a while. In November I started moving in a few salvageable belongings and some contributed items. Immediately I felt *at home*. I felt safe knowing Marsha and Tommy were next door. They had helped me through some tough days, weeks, and months. I'm glad I found a house beside them.

As time passed by, I stayed at home more and more. I just wanted to keep to myself. I stopped going to places I used to go, stopped hanging out with friends, stopped singing, and stopped playing my guitar. I have not taken it out of the case since before the tornado. I think the part of me that loved music so much disappeared that day, and I do not know if it will ever come back. My passion for music had died.

Going out to eat with co-workers, friends, or family, had become increasingly more difficult. I did not want anyone behind me at any time. I could not stand that, and it made me very uncomfortable. I needed a table against a wall so I would be in more control of my surroundings and have a clear view of anyone who might be approaching me. I have never really liked anyone sneaking up behind me, but now I am always on guard anticipating something that likely would not occur. Loud crowds drove me nuts. If the conversations got too loud or if children got too loud in a restaurant, I had to get out of there.

It was challenging at work for some of the same reasons. I got antsy if anyone was behind me, and sitting in a meeting or an all-day class was almost unbearable. I felt closed in, trapped with no escape route, thus causing a panic attack. Trivial things like someone typing on a keyboard sounded like they were on a jackhammer. My sense of hearing was so amplified that it drove me nuts. It was noisy in the plant where I worked. We built airplanes with lots of loud equipment clanging and banging. The exhaust fans in the huge paint booth very much resembled the high-pitched whirring of the tornado. Everything startled me. My guts stayed tied up in a knot most of the time, and I was on the verge of tears every day. Eventually all sounds drove me nuts. They were too loud! The one thing that was important to me was quitting time and getting home to my *safe place*, a place where there was no noise, no one talking, no one looking, no one walking up on my blind side, and I could have calm. I needed peaceful calm.

One day I received an email announcement about a tornado drill scheduled for the next day. I panicked immediately, and asked my boss if he knew what time the drill would be, and he said he would find out. It was scheduled for sometime around lunch or thereafter. I just knew that I could not be there. All eyes would be on the *tornado lady*, and I really did not know how I would react to a sudden alarm going off and a booming voice over the loud speakers saying, "TORNADO WARNING, SEEK SHELTER IMMEDIATELY!" I did not want to hear all the joking about it so I just took the next day off saving myself from all that. My boss said, "You want to take a day off because of a tornado drill? I guess I just don't understand PTSD." I stated emphatically, "I can't be here."

I COULD NOT BE THERE! What is the problem?? Why don't they understand this???

I am so tired of hearing people say, "I just don't understand it." I initially tried to explain it, but now I really do not care that they do not understand it. It is real, and it is ruining my life! I do not like it, but I have it, and I have to deal with it as best I can. I am looking out for me first from now on. People simply refuse to grasp what is not obvious.

Overwhelmed

Chapter 10: Job Sends Me To France

My job sent me abroad to France in July 2012. It was a great opportunity, and I was excited to go, yet reluctant. I needed to get away from my stressful job and away from the daily things that kept my guts tied in knots. Maybe a different venue would help me. I did not want to leave my *safe place* at home, but I went anyway. I primarily went to find out if that fearless, daredevil, I-can-do-anything girl that I used to be was still inside me somewhere. I just had to know. Could I hop on a plane with one-day notice and head off to a foreign country by myself? Is this a good idea or not? Other colleagues had taken the same trip, and I was generally not a person who would be outdone.

The trip went well until I had a panic attack at the Paris airport. I got off the plane, off the shuttle train, and suddenly a huge crowd was pushing me through the airport. I thought, "Holy crap, what is going on? Where are we going?" I could not get out of the mob; there were too many of them. Then I realized we were going through Customs. There I was totally engulfed in several lines going back and forth, crowds of people on both sides of me, behind me, in front of me, closing me in. I became very panicky, but the lines moved rather quickly. Before long, I was at Customs. I hoped I was not looking suspicious because I was so nervous and shaking. I had my passport stamped and proceeded to an open terminal with no more crowds pushing on me. Whew! I found my terminal and gate. As I waited for my flight to Nantes, I had a cold beer and tried to calm down.

Later arriving in Nantes, I had to wait 40 minutes for my luggage. Everyone was crowding around, pushing and squeezing in, to grab their luggage when they saw it. I finally got mine and retreated to the rental car office. I got my car, hooked up the GPS I brought with me from work, and prepared to venture on. First issue: the GPS said, "In 800 kilometers, enter the roundabout." Huh??? What the hell does that mean? How far is 800 kilometers? More importantly, just what is a roundabout? Of course, I passed right on by the roundabout, and the GPS said, "When possible make a legal U-turn." I did that, realized what a roundabout was, and entered it. The GPS said to take the second exit. Well, I could not take the second exit because of traffic in my way, so I went around the roundabout a second time to get a clear shot toward the exit I needed. That exit dumped me onto a four-lane highway with 40 miles to drive in order to arrive at my final destination in the town of Pornichet. The road symbols were different shapes, and I could not read the road signs in French. I did not have a cell phone with me although I had one waiting for me at work. I was thinking the entire drive, 'What if I break down or get lost? How will I get help? How will I communicate with someone? I don't speak French.' I was a bundle of nerves.

I was so relieved to find my hotel and park that *damn* car that I broke down and cried in the parking garage. I was a total wreck and literally had to pry my hands off that steering wheel! It took me a while to calm down before I could pry the seat out of my ***! Driving in a foreign country would be stressful for most people, but it really did a number on me. Whew!

On The Inside Looking Out

Pornichet, France

Overall, my four weeks in France went well. I had my moments at work and out of work. My workspace was in a large, open area. People were constantly moving about, frequently coming up behind me, startling me, and causing me to panic. There was no place to retreat even briefly for a moment of peace and quiet, and that definitely was not good. Away from work, the language barrier was a major hurdle. My limited ability to speak, read, or otherwise comprehend the French language was highly frustrating. Ordering meals in restaurants was difficult and annoying. I found myself using many hand gestures to communicate. Thank goodness, other colleagues from home were in the same boat. A few had been there longer than I had, and they knew what to order when we went out. I remained in my room most nights. It became my *safe place* away from home.

As the days passed, I continued to wrestle with the turmoil inside my head. Some friends from work offered to take me sightseeing, and I was determined to go since I was within a few hours of all the history. We visited Normandy, Omaha Beach, Utah Beach, Pointe du Hoc, and other points of interest, and that was quite peaceful. I am glad I had the opportunity to visit some of the places in France where my Daddy had been during his service in WWII.

Pointe du Hoc on the coast of Normandy

So peaceful... Will I ever find peace again ?

Chapter 10: Job Sends Me To France

Four weeks passed, and it was time to go home. My nervousness had escalated all day knowing I had to drive 40 miles back to Nantes. I arrived at my hotel across from the airport, checked in, and through my window spotted the rental car office. I decided to take the car over and return it so I would not need to do it the next morning. I drove around that airport three times before I could find a way to get into the rental car parking lot. I was getting more nervous by the second. Finally, I saw a car go through a small gate and followed it into the lot. I checked the car in, relieved to be done with it, and walked back to the hotel. By the time I reached the hotel, I was beginning to unravel.

The next morning I flew from Nantes to Paris, followed by a connection in Cincinnati, and then on to Raleigh. I was back in the USA! Jackie picked me up at the airport, and I headed home the following day. In retrospect, a trip to France was probably not good for me at this time in my life. It elevated my stress level more than I was prepared to deal with.

Chapter 11: Medical Leave

I arranged to see my therapist, Karla, immediately and told her of the good and bad experiences on the trip. The stress level at work had increased because I was way behind on things that needed attention after being away from my desk for four weeks. I felt as if I could break down and cry most days, and I knew I could not continue to live or work in this condition. I made an appointment to return in two weeks and got my prescriptions refilled.

When I went back two weeks later, I was not doing well at all. My nervousness had intensified, and I was hardly sleeping any at all. I was having more panic attacks and irritability, and I felt like something was crawling on me, but nothing was there. I was truly a wreck and on the verge of coming unglued. Karla suggested at this time that I take a medical leave from work, not for a few days, not for a few weeks, but for three months. She knew I needed to get out of that atmosphere and try to find some calm.

Three months medical leave passed without much significant improvement, and my mental and physical state subsequently resulted in long-term disability. Being away from the situation at work has helped by eliminating sudden loud noises, crowded meeting rooms, and the overall work-related stress and pressure that kept my nerves tied up in a bunch all day. I still have issues being around people, even family. Noises and my obsession with the weather are still very much a factor on a daily basis. I limit myself to time I can be around anyone. In the past I could work for endless hours on various projects until completed. Now my patience is gone, and I cannot concentrate on anything for very long. In order to accomplish anything complex, I need to take it in short spans and put it down for a while. It may take several days before I go back to it. I know what to do and how to do it. The knowledge is in my brain, but the thought process freezes and I cannot access the data. It will eventually unblock and flow again, and I will continue. I would describe it as a short circuit in my head. It took me more than a year and a half to write this book. I need to stay as peaceful and stress free as possible in order to be functional.

Chapter 12: Trying To Cope

I went through the routine of Christmas, cooked a big Christmas dinner, and had my family over. I did this primarily for my mother who has been fighting cancer for 17 years. I guess we all knew this would be her last Christmas, and I wanted to make it as *normal* as possible for her. Normal is not a word I use much anymore because not much is normal to me.

Thank God I did that because Mama passed away two months later. I had to *force* myself to go to the hospital every day to visit her. The elevators at the hospital were traumatic for me. If too many people started getting on, I would get off on that floor. I cannot stand being crowded or pinned in, and I can feel the anxiety building up in me. Being around anything depressing has a major effect on me, but I had to be there for her. I had to deal with her sickness and all the depressing things that go along with someone who is dying of cancer.

These on-going days of personal struggle caused me to have restless nights every night, more anxiety attacks, and more needing to be alone and away from people. I had to deal with the funeral and with a crowd of people wanting to hug and shake hands. The whole situation was out of my control, yet something I had no choice but to participate in. I felt so closed in that I just wanted to run away.

I was a country music singer all my life. For many years, I played before hundreds and thousands of people with no inhibitions. I enjoyed people, enjoyed the crowds, and enjoyed the attention. Mama wanted me to sing at her funeral, and I reluctantly told her I would. Yet when the time came to do it, I went into a major panic attack. I have not taken my guitar out of the case since before the tornado. I seem to have lost my love for music. I do not even play the radio much in my car. I am a changed person, and I cannot help it. On the day of the funeral, I almost backed out; but since it was Mama's final request of me, I could not refuse. I sang "Go Rest High On That Mountain", although I was very nervous. I was seriously afraid I would not make it through the song without cracking, but I managed to get through it somehow. Everyone said they did not know how I managed it. I dug way down deep and found the strength... for Mama. After all the hospital ordeal and funeral was over, I just kept to myself and did not want to be around anyone.

Chapter 12: Trying To Cope

Most days I stay right here at home and do not go anywhere. I have to choose the right time to go to the grocery store or run other errands. One grocery store nearby is good on Monday mornings. Very few people are there, but the main reason is that the cash register line does not box me in. It does not have candy and gum on one side and magazines along the other. It only has one rack of miscellaneous things on one side and wide-open space on the other. This is good because I cannot bear to feel trapped without an exit. I was never like that before, and I never thought about such things.

If I go to a restaurant, which is rare, I have to survey where I can sit. Most hosts do not like that, but I cannot help it. I need to have my back to a wall and be able to see the door. I need to know there is an escape route. I avoid crowds of people at all cost.

My older grandson had surgery at Duke in June, 2012. I told my daughter, Rebecca, that I would drive them to Durham, get a motel room, and be there with her for the surgery. Her husband stayed home with the other two children. I wanted to be there, I knew she needed me, but I knew two days would be about all I could deal with. My Aunt Becky said she would come up two days later to relieve me and bring them back home.

The hospital was very crowded. People were buzzing around everywhere, and there was nowhere quiet to sit. I took my earplugs with me in case things got loud and on my nerves. I used them several times. The waiting room was packed with people eating, sleeping, drinking coffee, looking at TV, reading books, and just being annoying. I had to walk away several times to scout out a peaceful spot, and there were not many to be found.

There was a water fountain in the main lobby. With the water sounds, this area was quite peaceful. I found myself going down there as much as possible. One time I was sitting there, enjoying the peace and enjoying the water, when a woman who worked there came over and asked if anyone was sitting in the seat beside me. I told her no, so she sat down and started scrolling through her cell phone. Obviously, this was a new phone because she had to swipe each screen so dramatically as to let everyone know, "Hey look, I have a new smart phone!" She did not just swipe with her finger to go to the next screen; she had to swipe as if she was directing damn traffic!

There I sat minding my own business and here comes this arm all in my personal space. *Swipe...* with a long dramatic extension of her arm as if she was pointing at something across the room. Then here comes another *Swipe....* with the same long dramatic extension of her arm. I thought, "What the hell? What is this all about? Jesus! Is there no peace anywhere in this entire hospital???" I got up and moved across the lobby to a quiet spot on the other side, and what happens now??? A man sits on the other side of a column right next to me and wants to check his voice mail... on the damn speakerphone! Once again I got up, rode the elevator down, and sat on a bench in the tunnel, just to have a moment of peace. By now I am at my wits end. It was a long day, the surgery went fine, and my grandson was doing well. My daughter was exhausted, of course, but wanted to spend the night at the hospital. I delivered up some dinner to her and then I left. I stopped by a steak house near by just to have a moment to myself. I took a seat at the bar and had a beer with dinner before going to the motel.

We left home on Tuesday at 7:00 a.m. The surgery was on Wednesday. Now it is Thursday, and I knew I needed to get out of there. I could sense my anxiety level increasing, my jaw clinching, and I was all but getting ready to fall apart. My aunt had said she would be at the hospital by noon. When she called around 1 p.m. to say she was in Durham, she also reported that her car had broken down. I was not very familiar with Durham; but thanks to a GPS, I managed to find her without a problem. We had to sit and wait for AAA to send a tow truck and follow them back to the garage. While we were watching TV in the waiting area, a weather bulletin interrupted to announce that bad weather was heading straight for us, and, of course, that caught my attention! The weatherman said it would be hitting Durham in 24 minutes. I just about freaked! I said to myself, "Oh my God, please not today! I cannot go through this again. I have to get out of here!!" I told my aunt that I was going next door to the Target store until the storm blew over and asked her if she wanted to go. She said she would just sit and wait there for her car. The weather report stated that 80 mph winds could accompany this storm. I was thinking as I glanced at Aunt Becky, 'This could be bad! How can you sit in this building with all these windows?' Aloud I asked her, "Are you sure?" And she calmly replied, "Yes."

Chapter 12: Trying To Cope

I hauled ass over to the Target store and found the aisle with pillows, blankets, etc., just in case something happened. It only took about 15 minutes for this rather intense storm to blow over, but I was in my own personal uproar!

My aunt's car was repaired during all this drama, and she followed me back to the hospital. I said goodbye and departed for Jackie's house about 35 minutes away. I spent the night there and headed for home the next day. I needed to get back to my safe place, my quiet place, my sanctuary. It took me about a week to recoup from all that. I simply cannot deal with stress without falling apart. I try hard to function and do things I need to do, but PTSD just changes everything.

Chapter 13: Living With PTSD

I continue to see my therapist, Karla, every two weeks. It has been nearly two years now, and I have no idea what shape I would be in without her. My life has forever changed. I will never be the person I once was. A mere weather report sends my mind into a frenzy. Any indication of a tornado watch or severe thunderstorm sets my whole system into a tailspin. We are experiencing unusual weather patterns all across the country. Tornadoes strike somewhere every week. I stay glued to the TV and cannot help it. I watch the broadcasts and see photos and videos of the aftermath of these storms. I know from my own experience what they went through, what they are going through, and what they will continue to go through. I also know their lives will be forever changed, and there is nothing they can do about it. I have accepted who I have become. I keep to myself and just try to survive day to day.

Go back to the symptoms I listed at the beginning of this story and read them again. You will see that many of these symptoms continue to affect my life. They are real. PTSD is real. There is no *magic pill* to make it go away. How I wish there were! You can talk to your family and friends about it, but they will not really understand it. More importantly, they do not want anything to be *wrong* with you. They want you to be the same person you were. They do not *see* anything wrong with you. As time passes they are less tolerant of the effects. They apparently think you should be past it by now.

If I had an arm or leg severed during the tornado, I would have a *visible* injury that people could actually see. They can see and empathize with that type of injury. It is the *invisible* wounds that people do not understand, nor do they want to deal with them for very long. God forbid you to have a "mental disorder." That is for crazy folks! I hear these sentences now: "Quit obsessing over the weather!" "Don't look at the weather report!" "Oh, thunder and lightning aren't going to hurt you!" "It's only a dark sky, not a tornado!" I have heard them all. Because of that, you begin to disconnect with people. You are tired of hearing all that crap. They do not have a clue what you are going through. It gets to the point that you do not discuss it anymore.

Thank God for my therapist, Karla! She has been my saving grace. I told her that if I had been badly burned, no one would walk up to me and light a match. They would not invite me to a bonfire and ask, 'Why are you afraid of this?' Fear is a horrible thing. I am not talking about someone walking up behind you and saying "Boo" or seeing a snake and being startled. You know how that makes you feel. Multiply it by 10,000, and that is how I feel most days, especially rainy, cloudy, and stormy days.

Being inside a tornado, hearing all those horrific sounds, and experiencing that brutal force created an intense fear that may stick with me forever! Been there, done that, got the tee shirt, and checked it off my bucket list! For anyone who has experienced a similar situation, I pray for your recovery. Please pray for mine.

The trauma that leads to post traumatic stress disorder is overwhelming and extremely frightening. Your sense of safety and trust are gone. Your mind and body cannot forget that time of terror. This keeps you on constant alert, and you are never calm. You cannot relax. There is no restful sleep. Because of this, you are exhausted all the time.

You cannot find peace and wonder if you ever will.

Some people never recover................

This piece of paper was found in my yard, torn from someone's hymn book.

It says, *"Jesus Is Passing This Way"*

It's framed and in my new home!

Conclusion

I titled this book "On The Inside Looking Out" because I know the person that I once was is still hidden inside me somewhere... constantly looking for safety... praying for the strength to emerge so I can be **ME** again.

Connie Owens

The End

About the author

Connie Owens has been a life long resident of eastern North Carolina. She has one daughter, Rebecca, and three grandchildren, Mitchell, Matthew, and Dakota. Connie was a country music singer/songwriter for many years. Today she is retired and enjoys working in her yard or relaxing at the beach. Sharing her terrifying experience and the aftermath of dealing with PTSD is important to her. She is very excited about writing this book and hopes it may help others better understand PTSD and the changes it can create in a person's life.

www.ingramcontent.com/pod-product-compliance
Lightning Source LLC
Chambersburg PA
CBHW060639290526
45793CB00001B/321